TABLE OF CONTENTS

Chapter 6 – Step 4: How to Attract the Customers You Love with Brand Positioning

- Why brand positioning is the most important decision you'll make
- Activity: how to create your brand positioning

Chapter 7 – Step 5: How to Make a Promise

- Why you need a brand promise
- Activity: how to create your brand promise
- How to create a KISS statement

Chapter 8 – Step 6: How to Name Your Business

- What mistakes to avoid in naming your business
- How to successfully name your business
- The pro's and con's of personal branding
- Activity: how to create a name for your business
- Activity: how to decide on your brand name
- How to finalize your brand strategy

Chapter 9 – The Five Brand Design Elements That Will Make You Look Like a Famous Brand

- What are the five brand elements will make you look like a famous brand
- How to choose a logo design
- Does your brand need a graphic element?
- What colour is your brand?
- What do your fonts say about your brand?
- What does your photography style say about your brand?
- How to take your brand to the next level

Chapter 10 – How to Hire for Logo Design

- What to look for when hiring a designer or branding agency
- Questions to ask a graphic designer or branding agency before hiring them
- Why awesome designers don't participate on (most) crowdsourcing sites

HOW TO GET THE MOST OUT OF THIS BOOK

A NOTE TO THE READER

Before you launch your business into the confines of the business world, and before you research the market viability of your purest thought, start writing your business plan, getting your logo designed and registering your URL I encourage you to start with the process in this guidebook. The steps will help you to unlock your creative genius and clarify your brand's purpose, vision, values, positioning, promise and name. This book will help you to breathe life into the power of your creation.

Why start with your brand? Three reasons. First, your business idea will benefit from your seed-stage creativity and help you to get clear how you're going to communicate your vision to the world. Second, your brand is the one plan you can always follow. Third, and most importantly, it will remind you of your authentic path in the context of the market opportunity and keep you true to your customer promise.

When you design your brand, you start with your life's purpose because, as the leader of your business, you are your brand. You may hire experts and consultants and collaborate as a team along the way, but the buck stops with you. As the Founder, you're the one who will stay awake at night wondering about the critical decisions you need to make.

It's my hope that your brand will help you sleep a little better knowing you're on a clear path. The clarity you gain through this book will ground your busy business mind in decisions you'll be proud of and help keep you on your envisioned path.

This book is a backstage pass to the mysterious and magical process of what we creative people do in our funky loft studios when we're masterminding your brands' existence. I've written it as a do-it-yourself guide for branding your business, but the topics I cover are equally as relevant for a funded startup who fully intends to hire this work out. Even if you decide to pay the big bucks to get your brand developed, any agency worth the money will dig deep with you into the questions we're going to explore in this book. For your brand, there's nothing more important than the clarity that can only be found in you.

In this book, I'm going to explain why your vision matters for your brand, walk you through each step needed to build a strong brand and then give you the tools you need to apply your plan to your startup immediately. You may be thinking, "but I'm not creative." Don't worry. I've developed lots of fun and pretty worksheets to give you an espresso shot for your imagination.

FOREWORD

I dedicate this book to every entrepreneur whose soul needs a spark of brandspiration.

I believe all of the solutions this planet needs are already here, and they are here, in you. Yes, you! The solution to issues like global warming, our food chain and healthy living can be found in anyone from our motorcycle-riding engineers to our hula-hooping doctors. Each person on this planet has a purpose.

Your purpose may have already awakened inside of you, or you may still be holding in a latent superpower that's yearning for your care and attention. All you need to do is listen to your intuitive zaps. Your purposeful path could come to you at any time. In a whisper, in a problem you see or in an ah-ha moment. Regardless of how it comes to you or what the idea is, I believe you deserve the tools to nurture your purposeful ideas into your profound realization. This book is a tool to ignite your entrepreneurial mission so that you can reach your dreams and connect with an audience that's waiting for you.

Cheers to the journey ahead and for the positive impact you will have on the world!

Bright love and gratitude,
Andrea xx

PS – Thank you for downloading my book. I'd be grateful if you would leave a comment on Amazon. I'm forever grateful. Thank you!

Chapter 1

WHAT TO EXPECT FROM THE BRANDING PROCESS

I'd sincerely like to acknowledge you for taking the first step towards building your brand. This step-by-step guide will give you the fundamental branding tools and worksheets you need to build your startup the way big famous businesses do it—the strategic way! In other words, the clear way that will stand the test of time and save you time, money and frustration. The steps outlined in this book are the secret ingredients to branding your business because your brand starts with you. Actually, the secret is inside you. Yes, that's right, YOU hold the answers to unlocking your brand's potential.

Branding is simply a process to help you unlock your passion while staying true to your authentic self

As an entrepreneur you may have zillions of ideas buzzing through your mind about how to communicate, what to do next and how to become famous. Think of this process as a way to organize your thoughts for your customer. Humans are organizational beings. The more you can do to communicate your thoughts in a simple way, the more likely your customers are to receive the messages you share with them.

If you follow the steps outlined in this book, you will be on the path to creating a brand that stands out from the competition and that you'll be extremely proud of. I guarantee that you'll learn a lot about yourself and your business as you go through this process.

The first part of the branding process is drafting statements that explore the five parts of your brand: purpose, vision, values, positioning and promise. These five parts are like the roadmap to help you ground the ideas in your mind into your brand and business concept before creating a name for your business and creating a logo design. Once you have gone through all five of these steps, your goal will be to finalize these drafts into concise statements. In doing these statements, you'll be developing a clear idea of the fundamental elements of your business brand.

If you've ever written a business plan you know that the moment you press save, it's obsolete. Here you are creating your brand's plan. It's the one plan you can always follow in your business and it's not meant to be fickle, changing from week to week, like your business plan might. Your brand is the foundation for being a leader with conviction, because once you have followed these steps you will feel clear and confident how to communicate your vision to the world. I promise if you commit to digging deep (real deep) you will find the clarity you're seeking. When you have a clearly articulated your brand the way you need to, how to lead the company will become clear. Your brand will help you make those tough decisions that keep you up at night. It will inspire you to start doing new things and to stop doing things that don't serve your vision. You will make decisions that you can look back on and be proud of. Your brand will remind you what matters.

Even if you're just thinking about starting a business, I recommend going through these steps before you name your business and getting your logo designed. I'll share more about naming your business and logo design in the later chapters of this book. It's so much easier to help a company when they're a blank slate than when they've already built a reputation, invested in a logo design and need a solution reverse engineered for them. The fact is, investing in your brand early means you most likely will avoid re-branding later on down the road when it's much more expensive and messy to resolve.

Before you can brand your business you will need the clarity this guidebook will help you find. All you need to do is make the commitment to do the work. Branding is an emotional process because it brings what truly matters about you and your business to the surface. It's possible you'll feel frustrated while you go through these brainstorming activities. That's normal. Stay loose and kind to yourself as you get started. Treat this as a work in progress.

The power of your brand lies in your ability to connect your business with your own passion and then relate that passion to your customers, employees and the world. Branding is the emotional side of your business, so expect to dig deep. It's more a matter of the heart than the head, but as you go through these activities, listen to both your head and your heart. Feel the answers. Trust your intuitive moments. If you get stuck, talk to others—mentors, friends, potential customers—with an open mind. Listen without an agenda. Be open. Be true to yourself, and most of all I want you to have FUN!

This book is about more than branding your business. It's about discovering your own potential to do Good in the world. Your customers want to connect with your business; they want to buy honest products and services from companies doing Good in the world. By following this process, you will learn how to create a partnership with your customers in which you both contribute to making the world a better place.

This step-by-step brand strategy process begins with a personal exploration of your own idea of doing Good in the world. We will be traveling into you and discovering what only you bring to this world. Don't be surprised if you encounter some blocks and negative thinking of yourself. "I'm not that special." "I'm just one person." "What can I do?" "I'm not gonna be the one who changes the industry." "I'm not a warm fluffy type—I've got a business to run." That is your negatively programmed subconscious talking. We've all got one of those. Just tell that mean monkey to SHUT UP!

You are creative, resourceful and full of Goodness! It's time to let your God-given gifts shine because you are unique. You do have a difference to make in this world, a legacy to establish and a market to serve. This is a time to be brave and to step into your strengths. The simple and soulful steps in this book will help you discover what makes you stand out so that you can lift your message up for your audience to hear.

If you're going to have a clear idea of what your brand stands for, then first we need to get intimate about what the wonderful world of branding is really all about. Quite frankly branding has a bad reputation. For starters, the most common misconception is that branding is all about the logo design, but that's like stepping out into the world with only your underwear on. Go ahead and laugh, but I see so many businesses doing it. Yup, they invest in only their underwear. You see, branding starts with who you are from within. Why you exist. Where you are going. How you behave. Who you attract. What you say. It's the consistency of all your brand's elements that creates a professional image for your company. When I refer to your brand's elements, I mean the brand messaging, colours, fonts, imagery and, of course, your logo that together create a cohesive brand image.

This guidebook is not about creating glossy statements that simply sounds good. It's about the clarity you will find as a leader by going through this creative process. Your brand is alive and will become powerful when it becomes embedded in your operational processes, behaviours and business decisions. It's much more than a few statements written on your "about us" page. The deeper you go, the greater brand power you will discover.

Brands don't fit in, they stand out

The activities in this book involve brainstorming. That means recording ALL of your thoughts, ideas and dreams down on paper without any judgments. There are no wrong answers! Nobody is looking over your shoulder so you don't need to be practical or even realistic. DREAM! And when you think you have it all down, go deeper, work harder.

DESIGN YOUR SPACE FOR THE CREATIVE PROCESS

It's your goal to leave this process with a brand that inspires your people, connects with your dream clients and contributes to the world. As you're going through this branding guide, I recommend that you create an inspiring space for these activities.

Here are some ideas to get you started.

IDEAS FOR SUPPLIES!

- Big paper
- Colourful marker pens

- Post-it notes
- Mentors, friends and colleagues
- Wine, water, coffee or tea
- Glue stick and scissors
- Courage
- Whatever you enjoy working with

WHAT TO DO TO GET YOU IN THE MOOD!

- Get out of your office or business
- Access your creative brain by doing something else—walking is a great activity, but so are cooking, doodling, photography and dancing
- Surround yourself with inspirational content

Your time is limited, so don't waste it living someone else's life. Don't be trapped by dogma—which is living with the results of other people's thinking. Don't let the noise of others' opinions drown out your own inner voice. And most important, have the courage to follow your heart and intuition. ~ Steve Jobs

Chapter 2

YOUR PERSONAL STORY IS INTEGRAL TO YOUR BRAND

The fact that I ended up in branding at all was a divinely inspired accident that resulted from a series of brave, nearing-on-insane decisions. When I graduated from University, I was itching to be thrown into the corporate deep end. I wanted a chance to swim, to prove myself, but I didn't know what I wanted to do. I felt out of sorts when I responded to the job opportunities in Canada. Too many requirements, and too many boxes to live inside. With $150 in my bank account I quit my well-paying, secure government job and headed off to Toronto in search of something to inspire my path. I ended up paying the bills working for a crazy making lawyer (because law school was an option in my mind), but I quickly realized that having my nose in a book all day and working 1700 billable hours a year wasn't my thang. Thankfully, an opportunity came up for me to pack my bags for Europe. My first project was in the opulent land of Dubai, and I pretty much never looked back. That's where I started my love affair with branding.

Turns out Dubai was all about swimming in the deep end. It gave me everything a young 20-something professional could ever dream of. There were helicopter rides, million dollar budgets, sea views, seven star hotel meetings, weekend trips to the Serengeti and, of course, Jimmy Choo. The studio I walked into everyday oozed creative talent, lessons learned and challenge. I I loved it and I got very good at swimming in the deep end.

I cut my teeth branding while managing eight major accounts simultaneously and exceeding yearly sales targets by 100% in six months. I was fortunate to spend one-on-one time with some of the gurus in the industry who invented branding. I've been the only unveiled woman flying to Kuwait on business trip to develop new markets I knew little about. I've facilitated intense full day workshop sessions with executive teams. I've seen mature men CEOs release tears due to the emotional depth of the branding work. I've had my pick of accounts to work on, re-branding everything from federal governments to luxurious hospitality groups. I've explored all of these things, which should have led to achievement and a sense of significance.

But all of this was only to learn that what I had been searching for was not what I really wanted. I was confused though because I did love branding. It's just that the work didn't leave me feeling full inside. I craved something more, but I didn't know what. Stupidly and totally ignoring my intuition, I accepted a job in London to work alongside another branding guru. In London the voice grew louder.

On my way back from facilitating a workshop for a global pharmaceutical company the tears started to pour down my face, and I knew something had to change. The pressure of pulling it all off had lifted, and the reality of my personal life and uninspiring new career choice was suddenly uncomfortable. I loved what I did; I just didn't feel an ounce of satisfaction working within the corporate world. Sprinkle in a bit of personal heart break, and I was on my way to discovering what would really fulfill me.

So, I moved home to Canada in search of something a little closer to my heart. Mountains, trees and the friendly Canadians.

It was in the rainy, lonely months that followed that my purpose finally hit me. I had been subcontracting to a branding agency in town and had been sitting in on meetings with startup entrepreneurs who wanted to make a difference in the world. The moment we'd start talking money in the tens of thousands of dollars range, I could feel their shocking disappointment as the three hour meeting would promptly come to a close. We'd later learn that they'd resort to buying a logo for a couple hundred bucks online or choosing an affordable freelance designer to work with. The problem I saw was that the logo was only part of what they needed. A logo design on its own was not enough to help these visionary entrepreneurs become world famous. I knew that they needed a way of connecting their message with their customers. They had a vision to share, an audience to speak to and a promise to make.

Their problem got me thinking. Our customers knew they wanted a logo; the challenge was that they didn't know what they really needed (clarity). Making matters worse, the industry was set up in such a way that the cost to get branded properly made the process inaccessible. This was a problem I felt called to solve at 12am one sleepless night. I literally got up and started writing down everything that was flowing through me.

I'll be honest: I had no clue how to solve this problem at first, but something inside of me had found the answer I had been searching for. I knew the solution would revolve around technology and providing strategic information freely. I also knew I'd have to find a way of attracting sophisticated western designers who understood brand identity work. But at that point, I wasn't clear exactly how I'd pull it all together.

This challenge gave me purpose in a way I never thought I'd find it. I certainly didn't ever picture myself developing a technology business. In the following months, I came up against plenty of my inner critical thoughts. They said things like "you're the last person who should be developing a technology business" and "you're not ready" and "how will you pay the bills; this is going to cost a lot to set up." Admittedly, I listened more to that inner voice in the early days than I did to the spark that had ignited my new found passion. In fact, I listened to it for more than a year.

But when I was told my contract was not being renewed because we simply didn't have the business to warrant keeping me on, I knew it was the universe's way of reminding me that I had something to do.

I share this with you because stories are how brands begin. Every time I'm working with a client one-on-one I'll take them back through their journey of starting their business. The journey leaves behind clues that help form the brand into a powerful story that your customers connect with.

Your story is unique to you. It will help you to establish why this new business idea exists in the first place and why you're passionate about getting out of bed in the morning each day. There will be clues in your story that will lead you to insights into the problem you're trying to solve with your business. It will even help you get clear about what kind of culture you don't want to create in your business. In the past, there are clues about the future you are about to create.

All our dreams can come true, if we have the courage to pursue them. ~ Walt Disney

need to connect to their emotional hot buttons.

Before we dive into your customers' emotional needs we must first tap into your own soul's purposeful path. As I've said before, as the leader of your business, you are your brand. I'd like you to think of your brand as an expression of your true authentic self.

Once we have tapped into your own purposeful path we'll explore how to inspire and connect with your customers. The goal of creating a brand is to create a connection with your customers. Your brand is the place to bring your passion to the surface so that it's contagiously noticeable.

Most entrepreneurs started their businesses because they saw a problem that needed to be resolved in the market. There are many different types of inspirations that might have initially sparked your idea to venture into the entrepreneurial world. Are you an industry challenger who is passionate about taking stale industries and disrupting them with your bravery like Richard Branson? Do you resonate with Blake Mycoskie of Toms shoes because you too feel a strong calling to create a for-profit business with a non-profit attitude? Or perhaps you're a heart-based entrepreneur like Oprah, and your path is all about enriching people's lives. Regardless of how your idea came to you, it's a gift and it could very well be your life's purpose. I believe your business is a platform for your good intentions to reach the world. It's an opportunity for you to live authentically, to make a difference and to put money in your bank account while doing something that you're proud of.

ACTIVITY: HOW TO CREATE A PURPOSE STATEMENT

Thinking about Your Purpose Statement

This step is essential for capturing your business's purpose as it relates to you, your customers and the world. Making money is satisfying and part of your business responsibility–you need to pay your rent and employees, deliver a product or service, etc. But I believe that needn't be your only purpose. Here I challenge you to explore the depths of why you're passionate about this business, why you cannot rest until this business has been realized.

We're talking about a purpose for your business that involves, empowers and inspires your customers, employees and yourself. You create a higher sense of fulfillment with your business, and your brand signals that to the world.

So let's get at it shall we? Not all of these questions will apply to you. Draft your responses to the questions that resonate with you. Let's start by brainstorming...

Brainstorming Questions

About your very own personal why

- Why are you personally inspired by this business?
- How will this business help you achieve your dreams?
- Why do you believe this business must exist in the world?
- Why are you passionate about resolving the problem you see in the market?
- What industry problem are you solving?
- How is your business contributing to the well-being of the people and planet?

It's important to also consider the voice of your customers. If you're going to create that meaningful connection with your customers, you'll need to develop empathy for your customers and truly understand their emotional needs.

About your customers' why

- What emotional needs are you fulfilling for your customers? Are you providing a means for them to overcome a fear? Are you helping them indulge in a desire? Are you inspiring them to reach their dreams?
- What problem does your customer have?
- How will your business help your customers play a role in contributing to the greater good?

About the greater good's why

- How is your business going to make the world a better place?
- How is your business helping the well-being of our people?
- How is your business improving the environment?

Writing your purpose statement

Some companies call it a mission statement, a manifesto or a purpose statement. They are essentially all the same thing. Use whatever sounds best to you, but whatever you call it, your startup's purpose statement is the reason why people will become raving fans of your business. Here you are creating an inspirational statement that will get YOU out of bed in the morning, but it should also inspire your customers and be the reason WHY they are choosing to buy from you too.

In the previous exercise, you brainstormed questions that inspire you personally and thought about how your business might relate that to your customers and the greater good. Now it's time to connect all three ideas together. Look for the common themes that have surfaced from the brainstorming questions. In your statement, you will want to communicate this common theme that links your business's purpose with you, your customers and the world. Your purpose statement is a wall-worthy statement. It belongs where your customers can see it. I'd also recommend having this in your "about us" section on your website.

Tips for writing your purpose statement

1. The statement should be personally fulfilling for you.
2. The statement should include how it will inspire your customers.
3. Finally, it should capture how your brand will have a positive impact on the world.

ACTIVITY: HOW TO CREATE BRAND MESSAGES THAT CONNECT WITH YOUR CUSTOMERS' EMOTIONAL HOT BUTTONS

Now that you've drafted your company's purpose statement I'm going to share with you how to avoid the mistake most entrepreneurs make in their brand messaging. As the founder of your startup, you're most likely a brilliant expert in your industry. The expertise you possess is without question your secret sauce, but when it comes to messaging, your expertise can be your worst enemy. I know this concept may be difficult to understand. I had a hard time with this notion too, but it's important for you to acknowledge that as an expert you see things quite differently than your customers do.

Let's take a Naturopathic doctor as an example. She has a high level of expertise that helps heal her patients. Let's say a patient comes into the doctor and says "help me with my digestive problem," and the doctor uncovers that the patient's high level of stress is what's causing his digestive problem. The patient WANTS help with his digestion, but in this case what she really NEEDS is to reduce his stress levels. As experts we often try to sell what we know our customers need, but in doing so we're missing out on a huge opportunity by not addressing what our customers want. In this case, the doctor needs to connect the dots between her patient's digestive problem and the potential stress solution. If the doctor wants to show her patient a meditation technique that reduce stress the brand message could sound something like this... "Heal your digestive problems in just 15 minutes a day."

Before we can truly empathize with our customers we have to forget everything we as experts know that our customers need. We have to let go of the knowledge we bring and step into the problems, aspirations and fears of our customers. We must intimately understand what's on our customers' minds, not ours.

Customers will buy from you based on the emotional promises you create. They choose to buy based on their emotions and then they justify it logically. The better you are able to resonate with your customers' emotions the more likely you are to sell them your product or service. It's simply a matter of packaging your message in a manner that makes your customers feel you understand them.

Thinking about Your Brand Messages

In this activity, we challenge you to step outside yourself and to step inside the minds of your ideal customers. In the first brainstorming section, write out an exhaustive list of your customers hopes, fears, desires and dreams. Ask yourself, what language do they use when they come to you? What do they say they want from you? What do they want to buy from you? Then once you can't think of any more, move down to the next set of brainstorming questions where you will be connecting your customers wants with what you know they need buy from you.

Brainstorming Questions

What does your customer want to buy from you?

- What solutions does your customer ask for?
- What does your customer fear?
- What does your customer have concerns about?
- What problems does your customer encounter?
- What goals does your customer have?
- What dreams does your customer have?
- What does your customer fantasize about?

TIP: Use your customer's exact language (not yours).

What does your customer need?

Now you can put your expert hat back on and look back through the previous list.

- What products or services do you provide that help customers overcome their fears or concerns?
- What products or services do you provide that help customers achieve their goals or dreams?
- What products or services do you provide that will help your customer live their fantasy?

How to Write Your Brand Messages

Now you can go back through your lists and create brand messages. All you need to do is go back through the WANTS and NEEDS lists. Connect the wants message in your customers voice with what you know your customers need. These brand messages can be used as headlines on your website, email subject lines, video titles and scripts, blog article headlines and so on.

Get instant access to the FREE branding worksheets here:

www.brandsfortheheart.com/brand-tools

Tom's is an example of building a company around a purposeful path

An excellent example of building a brand's story around purpose is Blake Mycoskie, founder of TOMS. While he was vacationing in Argentina he volunteered with a non-profit organization working to help poor children. He saw kids in a village with ragged old shoes or in some cases no shoes at all. He recalled a recent polo match he had attended in Argentina where the players wore a certain shoe called an "alpargata." Could these be a simple yet revolutionary solution for poor kids too?

Each one of us has a calling

Blake quickly set out to reinvent the alpargata as a stylish and comfy shoe for the U.S. market. But he had another goal—for every pair of shoes he sold, his company would donate a pair of shoes to a child in need.

Working together, the company and its customers began to take compassionate action to create a better world. During its first year in business, TOMS sold 10,000 pairs of shoes. Blake returned to Argentina later that year with family and friends and gave back to the children who had first inspired him. Thanks to supporters, TOMS gave its one millionth pair of new shoes to a child in need in September 2010.

TOMS now donates shoes in over 20 countries and works with charitable partners in the field who incorporate shoes into their health, education, hygiene, and community development programs. People love TOMS because it's a for-profit business model with a non-profit attitude.
TOMS One for One purpose has now spread to helping people with their sight when customers buy sunglasses.

Purpose Statement Example—TOMS

Personal Why: Helping the kids I saw in Argentina.
Customers' Why: My purchase helps a child.
The Greater Good: Helping kids live better, healthier lives.
Sweet Spot: TOMS One for One.

If we did all the things we are capable of doing, we would literally astound ourselves. ~ Thomas Edison

Chapter 4

STEP 2: HOW TO BLAZE A TRAIL IN YOUR INDUSTRY WITH VISION

WHY YOUR VISION STATEMENT WILL HELP YOU SAVE MONEY AND STAND OUT FROM COMPETITORS

Congrats on brainstorming a draft of your purpose statement! The next step will be easier now that you've considered how your business will change the world. Here we will brainstorm a vision for your business that will knock your competitors out of the water, help you save money and ensure you're purposefully directing your Good intentions. Your vision statement will help you be clear about the impact you envision making and how you will know when you get there. It's important to be decidedly clear about what you envision for the future of your company. It will help you make decisions that matter in achieving your goal. It will become clear what to start doing, what to stop doing and what to continue.

Your businesses vision statement is a long-term view of your strategic path, but most company statements fail to appeal to their customers. All too often companies' vision statements are written in a way that is self-serving for the company. Often I see and hear things like "we will become the leader in Y industry." Maybe this sounds familiar: "we will achieve X revenues" or "operate in A, B and C global markets." Instead of these common statements, we are going to uncover why your customers should care about your goals. As you learned in Chapter 4, it's important for your brand to connect on an emotional level with your customers.

The three benefits of creating a clear vision statement are:

- Branding once, not often (in other words, saving money!).

- Disrupting the market with innovative thinking.
- Aligning employees with measurable goals.

The visionary starts with a clean sheet of paper, and re-imagines the world. ~ Malcolm Gladwell

HOW TO ESTABLISH YOUR BRAND ARCHITECTURE FOR LONG-TERM GROWTH

Planning your brand's architecture is an important consideration in the early stages of your brand's development. Branding is a very expensive thing to change when you already have a presence in the market, signs on the doors, vehicle wraps and more. This is an important aspect of your brand to think through fully. If you're clear on your brand's architecture before getting your logo designed, your early clarity may end up saving you from re-branding down the road.

Imagine you're building your dream home. You'd have a plan right? Architectural drawings even. Before you broke ground, you'd know how many bedrooms and bathrooms you'd be building. You might be building a bedroom for an unborn child or even planning a basement you'll finish five years from now. You'd know what your family needed in the next ten years or so. Your type A planning mind would be in overdrive with questions, decisions and plans. Your brand needs an architectural plan too.

What I mean by brand architecture is how you structure and name the brands within your portfolio. Your brand's structure and naming strategy are how you create a relationship between your company's subsidiaries, products and services. The more brands you have the greater the marketing expenses.

Let's take Richard Branson's Virgin brand as an example. Virgin is an example of the most cost effective option for building your brand: the monolithic brand. Virgin competes in a wide range of industries, from airlines to telecommunication to fitness, all under one simple and powerful umbrella. In this case, the monolithic structure works beautifully for Virgin because their unifying elements are its brave messages and challenging ways. Branson believes that if they protect the integrity of the Virgin brand it has infinite possibilities. Apple is another company with a monolithic brand. Their naming strategy for their products is intentionally consistent; they have the iPhone, iPad, iPod, the MacBook Air, MacBook Pro and so on. This brand naming strategy groups Apples products together and creates strong product-level brands.There are two other main types of brand architecture systems. Endorsed is a system where all the brands are linked to the main business either by verbal or visual endorsement. Unilever is an example of this type of brand. Finally, we have freestanding, where the core business operates merely as a holding company, and each product or service is individually branded for its ideal client. An example of a freestanding brand is Tide, which is owned by Procter & Gamble.

Where you want to take the company should inform how you brand your company. It's important to start with a very narrow niche audience (which we will talk about in Chapter 7), but you need to be mindful of where you want your brand to be in 10 years. If you plan on expanding your products and services you may require an all-encompassing name to start.

On that note, let's talk about expanding your brand. When you develop a brand that is truly innovative, opportunities start to arise. While you're envisioning the prosperous future and growth areas, I encourage you to really stretch your thinking about what's possible. Creating your vision statement is an exercise for the imagination.

ACTIVITY: HOW TO CREATE A VISION STATEMENT THAT STANDS OUT

Creating the space for innovative thinking will help you get ahead of your competitors and stay there. If you envision a path that stretches you, you will start to think differently about what you need to do today to get where you want to go.

When your vision statement inspires your customers too, the sky's the limit. Your brand is a powerful opportunity to become the community architect and rally your tribe. Now, it's time to get your vision on! Let's get started.

Thinking about Your Vision Statement

Think of this activity as a platform that you have already created. I want you to visualize yourself there in the future having already achieved your far-reaching goals. Go ahead and imagine yourself in that place. The following questions are intended to spark your creative genius.

Brainstorming Questions

What does the future look like 5 to 10 years from now?

- How do you feel?
- Where are you?
- How do you spend your days?
- What knowledge have you empowered your customers with?
- What is it like to work in your team?
- What have you changed about the way your industry operates?
- What difference have you made in your customers' lives?
- How many markets are you operating in?
- What do the newspaper headlines say about your business?
- What financial goals have you achieved?
- How is your company contributing to the world?
- What's next?

How to Write Your Vision Statement

Once you have generated some ideas about what the future looks like, you will then need to commit to how you will measure your vision's progress. I recommend making those metrics specific enough so that your customers and the world can one day know that your vision has been reached. The most powerful way to articulate your vision is to define both a clear goal and a way to measure whether that goal has been accomplished. IBM had a vision to put a computer on every desk. Google is all about indexing the world's data. This language includes a measurable end goal. In essence, you should be able to pick up the phone and call me one day and say "I did it, it's done."
Remember what we discussed in Chapter 4 about relating your goals to your customers' goals and the greater good. Your vision statement should also speak to the future you envision for your customers' lives and the change your company will bring to the world.

Each one of us leaves behind a legacy

Try starting the sentences in your vision statement with the following:

- We will rest when...
- We see a world when...
- We dream of a day when...
- Together we will become...

Tips for writing your vision statement

1. It's a real stretch from where you are today!
2. It's so forward thinking and progressive that people think you're nuts!
3. It describes how your product or service will have a positive impact on your customers.

Reva is a good example of a visionary company that intends to positively impact the world. It's one of the first companies to introduce electric vehicles worldwide and to manufacture cars that are literally Born Green. Reva's vision is integral to their operations, from the manufacturing floor to the solar-powered battery in the car. The brand drives the way the company operates. I admire Reva because it's not just a car, it's a movement. We'll remember Reva for driving us into a petrol-free world.

HOW TO PUT YOUR VISION INTO ACTION AND TRACK PROGRESS

Once you have articulated your vision, it's important to translate that vision into the day-to-day activities in your business. Ask yourself, what are the three most important things you need to do within the next 30 days to take steps towards achieving your goals? (It's only three objectives at this stage because it needs to be implemented in manageable chunks.) Your vision will be achieved when you lead your company towards it. How will you align the company's activities and focus with your envisioned future?

Next, decide how you are going to measure these critical activities and which person is responsible for each objective and how you will report on the progress. Whenever possible, establish a way of tracking the progress of your goals. As a leader you will need to create rituals where you check in on a daily or weekly basis to measure your progress for each objective. Measuring your goals and tracking their success is essential for mobilizing your dream. I also recommend mapping out a long-term plan for achieving your objectives with metrics and assigning those objectives to the people accountable for them.

Chapter 5

STEP 3: HOW TO GROW YOUR STARTUP QUICKLY WITH BRAND VALUES

WHY YOUR BRAND VALUES ARE THE ONE PLAN YOU CAN ALWAYS FOLLOW

Have you ever thought "if only I could replicate myself in my business? If only I could hire another me?" If you've ever wondered how to bring more of you into your business and get the people you hire to behave the way you want them to, the answer starts with being clear about what you value. Openly stating your core values is how you operationalize your DNA into the behaviours of your business; these values will serve you even in the most difficult times. In this chapter, we'll be talking about how to grow your company quickly with values. If you plan on having a team of people, a partner or even doing a round of financing, then you'll want to be clear about what you stand for. You don't want to find that you've built a successful company but you aren't excited about coming into work anymore.

This is what happened to the CEO of NurseNextDoor.com, John DeHart. He started Nurse Next Door in Starbucks with his partner Ken Sim because they couldn't find quality home care for their families. Like many entrepreneurs they founded their business on a passionate purpose. On their road to growth, John walked into his office after being away for a few weeks and realized he didn't like coming to work anymore. He didn't like the way his supervisors spoke to their employees and customers. He didn't feel warmly welcomed into the office when he arrived back. It wasn't the kind of culture he wanted to belong to anymore. It made John uncomfortable walking into his own office. So he pulled his partner aside, and that was the day they decided things needed to change.

In fact, it was the beginning of a new era at Nurse Next Door that was based on what the founders valued. From then on, they vowed to be obsessed with their values because they knew that was the path to creating the company they had dreamed about in the early days. They made decisions about how to embody their values into the operational fabric of the company. The partners agreed to hire first and foremost based on their values. They would reward based on people's performance and alignment with their values. They would even bring their values to life in their weekly meetings. For Nurse Next Door, their commitment to their values have become a core reason for their incredible success. John now speaks worldwide on the importance of core values, and the company is one of North America's fastest growing franchises.

Values are key. They can be extremely powerful if they are constantly alive and referenced as part of your company culture. Values underpin the way people act and behave, they govern the way people are hired and fired, they define how policies are created and they attract like–minded employees and customers. They also inspire employee rewards and recognition, as well as the creation of new products. Very few companies tap into this business superpower, but the ones who do give a big high five to their values.

This step is about just that—core values—but I want you to articulate them in a way that's truthful. Values are the behaviours that underlie the way we act even when no one is watching: that's what I mean by telling the truth.

Values are who you are even when no one is watching

Corporate values often include words like integrity and excellence, but let's face it, customers don't believe that anymore. Customers are smart. They no longer believe everything they read or what they are told about a product or service. People talk to each other about what they like and don't like. How many stories have you heard about a disappointing customer experience? As a business you need to look at what you truly believe and what you can honestly deliver, and then you can commit to delivering those truths each and every day.

Customers are tired of generic statements that simply sound good. People are craving authenticity and transparency. Just look at how social media tools have empowered customers to have a conversation about your brand, with or without you. We can't hide behind managing perceptions anymore. It's time to speak the truth.

What would happen if we spoke the truth and consistently delivered on that experience for our customers and employees? What if we promised to behave in a way that we could actually live up to?

ACTIVITY: HOW TO BE CLEAR ABOUT YOUR BRAND VALUES

Before we talk about how to clarify your values, let's make sure we're on the same page about what values are. Here is how I define what values are and (equally as important) what they are not.

- Values start when we are children. Values are not a trend.
- Values are reality. Values are not ethics.
- Values are actions. Values are not a wish list. Values are not goals.
- Values are both the good and the less desirable sides of us.
- Values are the truth about who we really are. Values are not who we want to be.
- Values are what we say only when confirmed by our actions.
- Values are transparent. Values are not intentions.
- Values are present when people are watching and when they are not.

Thinking about Brand Values

Now that we're talking about the same thing, let's explore how to recognize what you value in and how to separate your values from your desired behaviours. I'll ask you some questions that will help guide you towards this clarity.

Brainstorming Questions

• What pisses you off?

Finding the truth behind what we value starts with getting intimate with what gets under our skin. You'll know when you're not living your values because you'll feel great discomfort. The opposite of what makes you uncomfortable is what you value. For example, if even a white lie makes you uncomfortable then you value honesty, transparency and telling the truth.

• What clues about your values are in your childhood?
Let's go back to when you were a child, because that's where your values began. You were taught certain behaviours at a very young age. Perhaps you were taught to say thank you and always show your appreciation. Who you were as a child has a lot to do with what you value today. Who were you when you were a kid?

• When you're a customer, how do you expect to be treated?
Look back on some of your own experiences as a customer. What experiences stand out in your mind as a customer? How was the service you received in alignment with who you are? Do you expect service to go above and beyond? Do you like it when you can do things yourself and save on things you don't need?

• What do your darkest moments say about your values?
Your values are with you even in your darkest moments, because values are not just who you wish to be. Values are how you behave in your most naked moments. How you act in these challenging times defines your values. Think back to the most difficult moment in your life. What did you do? What action did you take? And what was important about that action?

• What do your decisions say about your values?
Your actions say everything about what you value. How you hire, how you fire. How you compete with your competitors. Who you choose to date. What you eat. Why you launch new products and not others. All of your decisions, regardless of how small they may seem, say something about what you value. Are there some common themes in the decisions you make? What matters about the actions you took in those moments?

• What does your definition of success say about your values?
It seems Donald Trump values money above all else. You expect him to be a

leader who measures his employees' success by profitability and bottom line results. The polar opposite of that definition is a leader who defines his or her success by the positive impact being made in employees' and clients' lives. How do you define success? What does that say about what you value?

• What do your tweets and posts say about your values?
Your values are even present when you're posting and tweeting. Are you a big re-tweeter? Are you an information sharer? Are you a thought provoker? Are you a participant? Are you a listener? Are you a one-way stream? Every post is an action that embodies what you value. What does your communication style tell you about what you value? Your values are present in every moment of your life, from the simplest interactions like tweeting to your most challenging moments.

How to Write Your Brand Values
Once you have explored what you truthfully value then you will want to distill your findings into core themes. For example, if you value "doing things right," "nothing but the best" and "striving to provide the best" then you might want to bring all of these together in one theme. The simpler your values are to remember the more likely they are to be lived. I recommend articulating your values as mini-headline statements. You can even hast tag them on Twitter and speak to them in your social media to raise brand awareness about what you value.

Examples of core values from Nurse Next Door:

- Admire People
- WOW Customer service
- Find a better way
- Passionate about making a difference

For example, Nurse Next Door has tweeted to me in the past and used #admirepeople in the tweet. Values are an awesome social media conversation starter. It's an opportunity to architect a community of like minded people whose values are shared.

Feeling connected to each other is a basic human need. In fact, connection is the single driving factor behind our desires, fears, hopes and dreams. Naturally, everyone behaves in different ways, but it's our common values that bring people together in marriage and friendship. Values are how we connect with the employees we hire and even the companies we buy from. Values matter because they create connection.

Tips for writing your brand values

1. Choose 3 to 5 so that they are easy to remember.
2. Articulate your values with a courageous voice.
3. Write your values as mini-headines.

HOW TO PUT YOUR BRAND VALUES INTO ACTION AND TRACK PROGRESS

I recommend that you clarify ways to align your company's day-to-day behaviours with the values you have now created. Values are the foundation for your company's culture. People can no longer hide when your values are clear and visible. Once you have articulated your values, ask yourself what are the three most important behaviours the company needs to start within the next 30 days? (It's only three behaviours at this stage because your culture needs to be implemented in manageable chunks.) These expected behaviours will be necessary steps towards creating a culture that will help your company deliver on its promise to your customers. As the leader, you will model the way. Remember, values are not who you intend to be; they are who you are even when no one is watching. If the values you have articulated are accurate, the behaviours you implement should feel natural and authentic. You will need to decide how you are going to measure these behaviours and then check in on a daily (or weekly) basis. Following this alignment and mobilization of your values, I recommend mind mapping out a long-term plan with more ideas on how to create the culture you want both quickly and over the long term.

WHAT HAPPENS ONCE YOU HAVE DEFINED YOUR VALUES

When you start to become aware of your values you will become accountable for the business you value leading. You will consciously design how each day happens; life no longer will just happen to you. But remember, you're human and you'll make mistakes. People, businesses and products are not always perfect. Mistakes happen. What matters the most is how you handle your mistakes.

Have you ever been faced with a situation where confronting someone is more difficult than ignoring them? Have you been in a situation where the truth would be a difficult pill to swallow? As a result, do you end up taking the easy way out so that you or your business won't look bad? Let's take the value of honesty as an example. If you value honesty (like so many companies claim) then you should confess the truth regardless of the outcome or monetary loss, but we both know that doesn't always happen. People take the easy way out all the time.

The question you will need to ask yourself here is how uncomfortable is the easy path to take? If it makes you terribly uncomfortable, then you clearly value honesty and you may choose to find a graceful way to courageously speak your truth.

The moment you compromise your values you let a piece of you slip away. If it makes you feel uncomfortable, then stand in the discomfort. You might just be pleasantly surprised at the long-term effects of living in your values. Clarifying your values could be the best thing you've ever done personally and professionally because you will feel clear.

Chapter 6

STEP 4: ATTRACT CUSTOMERS YOU LOVE WITH BRAND POSITIONING

WHY BRAND POSITIONING IS THE MOST IMPORTANT DECISION YOU'LL MAKE

Brand positioning is the most important decision you'll make to help your startup become famous the way you envision. Ironically, it's the most challenging decision I guide entrepreneurs through.

Positioning is about why customers will choose you above the competition. In this step, we will discover who you want to attract and why your product or service is truly unique. When I start this conversation with clients they often tell me "we have the best quality," "we offer the best customer service," "we are the best" or "we are the most unique."

Here we need to dig much deeper than words like "best," "quality," "unique" and "customer service." We need to get specific about you and your business. It's time to be brave.

As a startup you can't afford a target market. What you need is a clearly articulated competitive advantage and an ideal client to sell it to. Starting with this narrow focus will help you intentionally build your reputation. It will shape what people say about you and how they spread the word. "Chilwin is the straight–talking lawyer that helps tech startups." "Dr. Dani helps the busy modern woman with digestive problems."

Your startup will stand out when you're brave about what you sell and who you sell it to. Typically, people try to be all things for all people in hopes of getting some customers, when in fact you need to be brave enough to avoid certain groups. By focusing on the customers you want to serve, you concentrate your energy where it needs to be. It's ok to exclude certain customers. Sometimes we have to say "no" to create the space for saying "yes."

When you're just launching your niche it should be uncomfortably narrow. I say this because most often it makes my client feel uncomfortable. If you want to sell to people between the ages of 30 to 50, you'll need to get way more narrow. Instead, I'd like you to imagine if you could only speak to one client. How old is this person? Are they male or female? What lifestyle choices do they make? What do they do for living? Where do they shop? This doesn't mean you will only have one customer or that you will be limited to this narrow niche forever, but it's how you will ignite your presence in the market.

Imagine you're building a fire. Would you start with the biggest log? If you did, would the fire burn? Likely not. Your common sense tells you to start with a small fire and then build it bigger once it's already burning. The same methodology applies to igniting your market. Start small, with the right ingredients, and then gradually build the fire from there. Gabrielle Bernstein is a writer, vlogger, speaker and coach who is quickly becoming the next generation's Oprah. She openly shares her personal journey of leaving behind addiction and moving towards a healthy spiritual life.

Her books *Spirit Junkie* and *Add More 'Ing to Your Life* speak to the style–conscious, 30–something woman seeking more out of life. Gabby openly shares her life experiences, talking about spirituality in a way that is most relevant to the next generation of women.

Gabby doesn't worry about speaking to everyone even though baby boomers and professional men might be drawn to her too. Instead she focuses her conversations for her fast growing gal-pal tribe. While you may think this approach is limiting her growth, it didn't stop Google from having her do a speaking gig for their employees.

That's the power that comes from stepping into your authenticity and being brave about who you are. You become famous for something specific and you attract like-minded customers.

ACTIVITY: HOW TO CREATE YOUR BRAND POSITIONING

Thinking about Brand Positioning

In this activity, you'll explore what you want to be famous for and determine what reputation you
wish to build for your business. It's important to be authentic here too. It matters that you are passionate about the customers you will be serving. You will also need to check that the audience will be profitable for your business. In the following activities you will be exploring your ideal client. This customer should inspire you to step into your brave voice. Everyone has superpowers; it's just a matter of finding the right audience for them. The goal here is to STOP competing with the competition.

There is only one you in the world.

The goal of this activity is to paint a picture of who you are selling to or, if you're business-to-business, what industry you're selling to. The goal here is to align who you are selling to and what you are selling to create a sweet spot for your brand's positioning.

Brainstorming questions

Who are you selling to?

- Who will buy your product or service?
- Add a demography or lifestyle choice. If they're business-to-business, what industry do they operate in?
- Are they male or female? What position do they hold?
- Where do they live? Where is the business located?
- Keep asking yourself questions to become clear about exactly who you are selling to.

What are you selling?

- What category or industry are you competing in?
- What area of expertise or specialization can you bring?

- What is it that only you provide?

Now I'd like you to double check that what you're selling and who you're selling it to are in fact unique. I'd like you to draw a strategy canvas.

Start with a graph with an X and Y axis. Write down a legend with a list of all your competitors. Then label categories on the X-axis that correspond to differentiators such as markets they serve, price point, product, service offerings, etc. Label the Y-axis 1-10, and rate each company, including your own, by marking them an a scale of 1-10 in every category. Lastly, connect the points for each company. Your line should have a dramatic difference then your competitors in at least one area that your customers actually care about.

How to Write Your Positioning Statement

Your startup's positioning statement is most often used internally and in pitches to help explain what you sell and who you sell to. The most important part of positioning your brand is for you and your team to be clear on who to market to and how to communicate what you're offering. It does not necessarily need to be an externally articulated statement.

Tips for getting clear on your brand positioning

You'll know you have nailed your positioning when...

- You have an intimate understanding of WHO you are selling to.
- Your competitors would be jealous if you went to market with this strategy.
- Your colleagues think that you're crazy because it's so specific.
- None of your competitors are doing it.
- The described market is not currently being served.
- People will talk about it, because it IS different.
- It gives you ideas about what touch points your brand should have.
- It helps you find your audience.

Chapter 7

STEP 5: HOW TO MAKE A BRAND PROMISE

WHY YOU NEED A BRAND PROMISE

Some call it a Tagline, others call it a Slogan. Whatever you call it, a brand promise is that key phrase that belongs on your business card, website or t-shirt. It captures the promise your business is making.

Your promise is where the rubber hits the road: it communicates what your business is about. It's a great opportunity to make your customers smile, make them think or give them a taste of what to expect from your company. This phrase should pull at the emotional chords of your customers. It should reach the customers you intend to attract. This promise is most powerful when it's the truth.

Best to under-promise and over-deliver than to disappoint a single customer.

Companies like Apple have spent millions to create an arresting brand name and promise. Obviously, Apple has nothing to do with selling fruit. It's become the name that people associate with a tech-savvy lifestyle. And the promise "Think Different" says how they run their business and how you can run your life using their products.

How can you do this for your own business? It's a process that requires both the head and the heart. So we are going to brainstorm ideas from the heart to create an emotional link with your customers, and we'll analyze with your head how you might deliver that link with your product or service.

Don't block yourself by thinking that your name or promise has to do all this work on its own. All the aspects of your brand work with each other and with the reputation you create. They will be in your customers' consciousness every time they drink your coffee, buy your book, visit your website or walk past your shop.

When I was going through this process for my own business I explored several names, all with the word "brand" in them: Brand Match, Next Brands, Purpose Brands (plus about 46 others). I also had a list of promise statements, all using words like "Good," "people" and "connect." I got so frustrated I let it go for a few days. Later, when I came back to my lists, I saw Brands for the People, which I instantly loved as both a name and a promise.

ACTIVITY: HOW TO CREATE YOUR BRAND PROMISE

When you were a kid did you ever play a game of telephone? One person would start with a phrase and whisper it to the kid next to them. Once the message traveled through all the kids in the circle, the last person would say the statement aloud, and it would sound completely different from the original phrase. This confusion is what we want to avoid for your brand. It sounds like a simple concept, but it's surprising how many leaders I have spoken to over the years who lack this clear and coherent understanding about their brand internally. If the confusion is happening internally, then without a doubt it's confusing customers too. Clarity and cohesion is a must have for successful branding.

A great way of creating your brand's essence is to distill down everything we have covered in the previous chapters of this book, including your purpose, vision, values and positioning, and simplify it into a straightforward statement about your brand's idea. The core essence of your brand is an internal statement, so you don't have to worry about making it sound delicious quite yet. To help you with this, I'd like to share an exercise to peel back the layers of the onion to get to the core of your brand idea.

Thinking about Your Core Essence

Ask yourself what's your brand's core idea? And then say, no it's not that. Then ask the question again and again. Do it at least five times. You can try asking different questions if you like. For example, I want my business to be known for... The goal here is to come up with one word or a short phrase for your brand's core idea.

The brand idea is_______
No it's not that....
The brand idea is_______
No it's not that....
The brand idea is_______
No it's not that....
The brand idea is_______
No it's not that....
The brand idea is_______
No it's not that....
The brand idea is_______
No it's not that....
The brand idea is_______

Thinking about Your Brand Promise

Now that you're clear on the internal core essence of your brand we can begin to explore your juicy promise statement. Using the categories below, create a list of the basic content of what your brand promise needs to say. What words do you wish to associate with your brand promise? Once you have the basic words articulated, then start brainstorming new words, new ways of using those words and new approaches for communicating the basic content. Have fun with this, record everything and remember there is no such thing as a bad idea!

Categories for your promise statement:

- Words about what you do
- Words about how you do it
- Words about your point of view
- Words that capture your personality
- Words about the Good you're doing

I love these brand promises:

- Ethical Bean: Just. Better.
- Reva: Driving you into a petrol-free world.
- TED: Ideas worth spreading.
- Springwise: Your essential fix of entrepreneurial ideas.
- Innocent: Little tasty drinks.
- De Beers: A diamond is forever.

Tips for creating your brand promise

How will you know your promise is brilliant?

- It makes you smile or challenges your thinking.
- It captures your personality and attitude.
- It makes you nervous because it IS different.
- It's succinct—every word counts.
- It's memorable.
- It uses a double entendre (means more than one thing).

HOW TO CREATE A KISS STATEMENT

Now that you've drafted your brand promise you may decide that you need a "Keep It Simple Stupid" statement. If your company name does not communicate what you're selling and your brand promise doesn't communicate it either, then you will need one of these. For example, the name Apple doesn't communicate what they sell or do, nor does their promise "Think Different." In this case, if they were a startup I'd recommend they have a statement that communicates these things to an eight year old, a statement like "Electronics for Modern Living" or "Technology for Cool People." Nothing too clever, just simple and basic communication. If you need one of these, I'd recommend placing it on your home page, business card and other branded elements.

Chapter 8

STEP 6: HOW TO NAME YOUR BUSINESS

Naming your business can be a tricky process as there are many moving parts to consider in making the right decision. Firstly, it can be a very emotional process for business owners to navigate through to find a name that they love, but there are also critical logistical considerations that cannot be overlooked. In this chapter, I'll share with you what I've learned so that hopefully you don't have to experience the monetary and reputation costs of having to change your business name later on. All to often, I see startups that end up having to change their business name when they are already a few years into running the business. So, let's make sure we avoid that pain for you.

Develop your brand strategy first

Firstly, before you name your business I highly recommend that you go through the previous Chapters 3 through 7 to develop your brand strategy BEFORE choosing your business name. When entrepreneurs think about branding their business they often think first about needing a business name and a logo design, but jumping into these decisions is like marrying someone after the first few dates. Like marriage, these decision will impact your future in different ways that must be strategically and carefully considered.

Imagine if Amazon.com wasn't clear on their vision (see Chapter 4) before naming their business. If that happened they might have ended up calling Amazon something descriptive instead like OnlineBooks.com, because that's what the business niche was catering towards at the time. It's can be frustrating to choose a name if you have more then one decision maker in the mix, because everyone has an opinion to offer when it comes to naming your business. Your brand strategy will help you ground your teams opinions into what's right for the business plan and brand. The brand strategy will give you an objective perspective, while helping you feel clear and confident about what is, and what isn't a good name for the business.

Furthermore, going back to the Amazon example, if they called it onlinebooks.com this descriptive naming approach would have been a limiting name for their long-term growth into other segments such as electronics, clothing and beauty care. Instead Amazon strategically choose a non-descriptive name, which allowed for their future expansion into new and highly profitable revenue streams, without having to go through any painful name changes for their business. It may take a more time, but as you can see creating a brand strategy is valuable to ensure all the business implications rather then waiting until it's too late.

Make it easy for customers to find you without creating confusion
Choosing the right name for your business can be cumbersome in todays digital world, because your business name extends far beyond the borders of your city and country. The of which will become clear with competitive research and trademarking registration.

Trademark issues also need to be taken into account not only locally but also internationally. Many companies that apply for Trademarks also sign up to monitoring services where they watch out for similar business names being approved in other countries. If the company can prove that they have clients in your country and they have done adequate promotions in your markets then they may be able to prove that they have the rights to use the name before you do. The problem is that you don't always find this out about them until your business is launched and you're engaged in the Trademarking process.

Trademark disputes are common with descriptive names because it's the most common way to name a business. Descriptive names also creates more confusion for customers. For example the dentist industry is a great example of the word "smile" being over used in business names as it describes the benefit that most people are seeking when hiring a dentist. Other over used words for business names of social enterprises includes words like eco, green, organics, sustainable and more. For this reason, descriptive business names are the most problematic for Trademarking because they leave room for the greatest deal of confusion for customers.

If Trademark disputes are not a solid enough reason for you to avoid using a descriptive type of name for your business, it's worth considering the effects a descriptive name will have on your business name's Google search. When I googled "smile dentist" I got 19,600,000 results and pages were filled with results of business names using both the word smile and the word dentist in them.

When naming your business the goal is to make it easy for your customer to find you, so when a friend refers your business to a potential new customer and they google you, they will find you right up on page one in their search results. For these reasons alone, I'd recommend avoiding descriptive business names, because quite frankly they have a tendency to bring on a few headaches.

What we can also learn from Amazon's approach to naming their business is that the type of name they choose has stood the test of time and multiple markets. Amazon is an out of the box name like Apple, Twitter, Yahoo. Infact, the technology industry has started a new trend of these non-descriptive types of business names. These types of out of the box names require a bit more effort in terms of your creativity in your branding and clear messaging, because it's not immediately obvious what your company does and sells; however, these types of names are far easier to trademark and have less Google competition. For best results, you should hire a Trademark Lawyer or Agent and also conduct Google research to see for yourself if the naming ideas you have been used in your industry.

Furthermore, you want a name that is memorable and easy to pronounce. Before deciding on a business name, test it by sharing it with friends and family. In the activity below there is additional information about how to decide on the right business name.

The pro's and con's of personal branding

Over the years, there has been an explosion of new websites online. Many bloggers started with a branded company name and then eventually ended up using their own personal brand name. A personal brand name may or may not be right for you. Here the pro's and con's for personal branding to help you decide if this is the right direction for your new business.

Pro's for personal branding

- People like to do business and buy from real people
- It allows your message to grow and evolve as you do
- It keeps you and your authenticity at the core of your business
- If you have a unique name it can be virgin territory on the internet
- It's a great option if you want to establish personal credibility
- You can establish the like, know and trust factor faster

Con's for personal branding

- If you're building your business to sell it then choosing a personal brand is not your best choice (unless you don't mind changing your name😃)
- It can be challenging to scale the business for high growth because your customers may want to have direct contact with you
- If you get negative press it will follow you around like a bad smell
- You cannot afford to be shy if you have a personal brand
- If your name is difficult to spell it might be hard for people to find you when they search for you online
- If your name is common it may be challenging to carve out a unique space online in the google search
- If you're a private person a personal brand might not be the right choice for you

What are personal brands are best suited for?

1. Writers
2. Authors
3. Artists
4. Speakers
5. Professionals

ACTIVITY: HOW TO CREATE A NAME FOR YOUR BUSINESS

Here's an extra activity that will help guide you through the process of naming your business. Naming your business will possibly be one of the most challenging brand activities you'll embark upon because it can be an emotional decision and one that will say a lot about who your business is. But keep in mind that your name is just one aspect of your communication. In other words, don't pressure yourself to communicate everything in the name. Remember it's what you do with your name that will make it great. Because there are many aspects of a good name, the goal of this activity is to brainstorm as many ideas as possible. I recommend generating ideas for your brand's name in a few different categories unless you feel one of the categories is not on-brand for your business.

BUSINESS NAME CATEGORIES

Descriptive: Describes your products and services. For example: Whole Foods; British Airways; Bed, Bath & Beyond.

Personal brand: Uses founder's name(s) Dolce & Gabanna, Oprah, Madonna etc.

Perspective: Describes a philosophy. For example, Seventh Generation, Ethical Bean or Next Era Energy.

Conceptual: Words taken from ideas that relate to the product and service. For example: Nike (the goddess of victory), origin of company (Patagonia), or audience (Entrepreneur.com)

Invented: Newly created words usually made from two parts. For example: FedEx, Facebook, and Travelocity.

Outside of the box: Words that are random, playful and out of the ordinary. For example: Yahoo, Apple, and W Hotels.

Tips for Brainstorming:

- Use a Thesaurus to come up with lots of alternate words.
- Use Wikipedia to look up concepts that relate to your business.

- Consider word translations (for example, Latin, French, Italian).

ACTIVITY: HOW TO DECIDE ON YOUR BRAND NAME

Once you come up with various names, narrowing the list down can still be difficult. I recommend that you shortlist your favourites and use this activity to help you sift through your ideas. Rank each name on an effectiveness scale of 1 (lowest) to 10 (highest) using the following criteria:

Availability: Is the URL available? Are you able to register the business name? Try using www.networksolutions.com to see if your names are available.

Originality: Could the name be confused with any competitor? Check for the same or similar names.

Trademark: Can you obtain the trademark for the business name in all the countries where you are doing business.

Feel: Use it in a sentence. Is it memorable? Does it feel positive? Does it make you nervous (actually that's a good thing!)?

Sound: Use it in a sentence. How does it sound? Is it easy to read and pronounce? Is there a shorter version?

Consistency: Do people spell it the correct way consistently? Do people pronounce it the same way?

How to bring your brand strategy together

Now that you've drafted your brand strategy and come up with naming options, it's time to go back through the previous five steps (or six if you also needed to name your business) and make the brainstorming more polished and clear. Just remember, hardly anyone nails it the first time. Keep your thinking open. Don't let that saboteur talk you out of anything! Once you feel you have articulated your ideas clearly in your drafts, try them out on your friends and colleagues. Be curious about what they like and why as well as what they don't like and why. Keep an open mind. Just record their reactions.

Now comes the easy part. Try to let it go for at least 24 hours and do something completely different. Then come back to it. You may be surprised at what stands out or sounds ordinary when you come back to re–evaluate. It's tempting to skip this step if you're on a deadline, but it's essential. The statements and business name you are making are the foundations of your business and, of course, your brand.

Once you have gone through the rough draft process, make sure to complete your final statements. It's important that you make a commitment to achieving clarity in the process you have just gone through. I recommend making some of these statements visible to your customers, especially the promise and values.

And when you hire people, show them this page. Talk to them about your purpose, dreams and the unique business culture you are building.

Chapter 9

THE 5 DESIGN ELEMENTS THAT WILL MAKE YOU LOOK LIKE A FAMOUS BRAND

So, you're bootstrapping your big idea and you want it to take off and become famous so that you can make a positive impact in the world. You value the importance of branding because you appreciate that it will help you look professional and put your best foot forward into the world, because you only have one chance to make a first impression. In this chapter, I'm going to share how you can successfully brand your business so that it looks like your company is a multi-million dollar business right out of the gates.

The five brand design elements:

1. Logo design
2. Graphic element
3. Colour palate (primary and secondary)
4. Font palate
5. Photography style

If a picture is worth a thousand words, then these five elements form those visual cues that convey the thousand word message about your brand. Designers call these five brand elements 'the visual language' and these elements are what brings your brand strategy to life. These visual elements are intended to be used consistently over-time, because they all work together in harmony to establish the look and feel of your brand. Therefore, delivering your brand message successfully relies on your ability to bridge the gap between all of these elements to your audience through a consistent visual system.

1. How to choose a logo design

Perhaps one of the greatest mistakes I see entrepreneurs making with their logo design is that they try to communicate everything about what the company does in the logo design. However, when you look at famous brands like Apple, Nike and Starbucks these logo designs don't actually say what the company does, sells or creates in the logo. What does an apple have to do with computers? The swoosh have to do with athletic attire? And the mermaid woman have to do with coffee? Nothing. These symbols are the big idea or concept that builds a story that attracts customers and establishes competitive differentiation. On the other hand, many famous brands don't even have symbols like Jeep, Cannon, Virgin and Facebook. When you're developing a famous brand, model the best and don't worry about saying it all in the logo design, that's where your brand strategy and other visual elements comes into play.

With logo design, simple is always better. A complex logo with various colours and visual elements can be difficult to reproduce at small sizes and on different surfaces like T-shirts or exterior surfaces like metal. Complexity can create legibility issues too which can lead to gumming up or smudge together when reproduced in small sizes. Also, if the logo has a complex symbol it may be difficult to use at a large size like on store front signage.

Complex logo's quickly start to look dated. You will notice that famous brands logo designs get simpler over-time. The Starbucks brands, for example, has evolved from the twin-tailed siren woman sketch into a far more simpler version of the drawing. In the most recent re-branding in 2011 they actually separated the symbol from the wordmark and removed the word coffee, all for the greater good of simplicity.

I've seen entrepreneurs bootstrapping that turn to methods like downloading logo templates or worse clip art. While you may be saving money doing this, it's far from a good idea, because it's never going to be original and its possible customers won't take you seriously. If you're that cost conscious, create a logo design that is simply a font and keep your logo design typographic for now. Less is more when it comes to logo design.

Also, your tagline or brand promise should have a relationship to your logo design, but it should not be a part of logo design itself.

Once you have decided on your logo design, don't change it unless you have a business case reason to do so. In other words, just because you now prefer a different style or colour is not a reason to change your brand's system. If you have gone through the branding process with excellence and depth then you shouldn't have to change the logo design.

2. Does your brand need a graphic element?

The Nike swoosh is an example of a graphic device used prominently in a brands visual language. This could be an element that is derived from your logo design or it could also be an additional element that works in harmony with your other visual elements. Some brands use mascots like Ronald MacDonald, the Twitter bird or the Michelin man. You may wish to consider having one of these for your brand, but it's not a must have.

3. What colour is your brand?

If you saw a photo of a little blue box with a white ribbon around it, what brand would you think of? When I ask this question to a crowd full people the women immediately reply by saying "Tiffany's". That's because that robins egg blue is synonymous with the Tiffany's brand and even though you can't see the logo on the picture I show them that little blue box symbolizes the Tiffany's brand.

Similarly, the courier industry prominently uses colour as a differentiator too, to the point that if you see a brown truck you will immediately know it's a UPS truck. In essence, colour has been used prominently by some of the world's most famous brands and it's highly worth considering what colour you want your brand to be.

The colour(s) you choose for your brand are inextricably linked to physiological cues about your brand. One of the most common colours for brands is blue, because it's men's and women's favourite colour. Infact, 33% of the top brand use the colour blue in their logo. The colour blue holds positive connotations such as being professional, loyal, confident and calm. Yellow on the other hand is perceived as happy, optimistic and joyful and red symbolizes strength, passion, courage and safety.

In other words, colour communicates and our minds are programmed to respond to colour. Research has shown that 90% of people will establish snap judgements about a brand based on colour alone.

The other thing you might want to consider when choosing a colour is what colours are your competitors using. If they are all using blue then perhaps you want to choose a different colour that will help you to bravely stand out from the crowd.

You may also wish to consider a secondary colour palate for your brand. This will especially come in handy if you have lots of information design needs in your business or you offer various product offerings.

4. What do your fonts say about your brand?
Font is also another powerful visual expression tool. Like colour, typefaces have personality too and it's important to also keep in mind that the colour you choose will interact with the fonts you choose. Together, your fonts and colour will form a message.

Fonts are categorized into either 1) Serif or 2) Sans Serif. Serif fonts have feet in the letter forms (ie: times new roman) while sans serif fonts don't have these feet (ie: arial). Therefore, serif fonts have a more classic or traditional feel to them whereas sans serif fonts have a more modern or futuristic appeal.

Also, the way you use a font communicates too, therefore if you are using all UPPERCASE it has a solid, strong, masculine appeal; italics on the other hand represents movement or brings attention to the content.

When establishing your font palate, choose a family of fonts approximately two to three fonts that you will use for the following purposes:

- Headlines 1
- Headlines 2 / Subtitle
- Headlines 3 / Subtitle
- Body copy style
- Pull quote style

- Bullet style
- Button style

Overall, it's imperative to choose fonts that are legible and easy to read especially with your body copy, because the eye may tire if it's too difficult to read.

The love Is In the details.

5. What does your photography style say about your brand?
It's necessary to have a photography style for your brand that you use consistently if you want to create a famous brand and yet this is the one key branded element I observe many entrepreneurs missing. Photography is such a large part of the way any brand communicates these days, because imagery drives social media engagement. This may sound a little harsh, but it's for your benefit, but when you use 'me-too' images you immediately fade into the clutter and look like a small business. What do I mean by 'me-too' images? Essentially, I'm talking about those obvious images that you see on everyone's blog, direct mailer. They are the images that you have seen a million times that communicate a literal message like the woman sitting on the beach or the two men shaking hands.

Many of the big brands, invest heavily in photo shoots, stylists and creative directors to capture the perfect image style for their brand. Pay attention to some of your favourite brands and observe their photography style. For example: Telus is a telecommunications company in Canada that uses various animals and flowers on a white background. If you saw a billboard with their white background and a lizard (even without seeing the logo) you'd immediately know what company it was.

The good news is that there are inexpensive ways to achieve a similar result using image libraries like www.veer.com or www.gettyimages.com and many others. You can often find image collections on these sites that pull together a unique and consistent style. Consider starting with an image concept that you feel illustrates the personality of the brand.

Have fun with it and try downloading one of the many different photo apps like Instagram or Hipstamatic. Create your own consistent style using one of these filters and with your own photography.

How to take your brand to the next level

Throughout this book, I have been advocating the importance on having a strategic platform for your business before turning your attention to the logo design. Apple is a great example of a brand where their brand personality, vision, values and promise are brought to life not only in their logo design but on every touch point ranging from retail environments, product design, website design, interface design and so on. The brand is embedded into the companies DNA.

Apple is about imagination, design and innovation and you can see how this comes to life in their clean-cut, modern design and humanistic approach to technology. Design has been considered down to every last detail. They even have their own apple typeface. I invite you to aspire to this level of brand integration across your business.

"Design Is how It works" – Steve Jobs

Ideas for how to integrate your brand elements like a pro:

- Use your fonts, colours, brand promise and social media links in your email signature
- Wear one of your brand colours for your profile photo
- Create video's using your brand's colours in the background video's
- Create quotes using your font styles and colours to share on social media
- Integrate your visual language into your store or office environment
- Next time you hire someone try to create behavioural based questions to determine if their personality aligns your brand values
- Come up with a free giveaway for your customers
- Create a reward around living your brand's values. Allow people to nominate each other and capture stories about how you have brought your values to life with customers or internally
- Develop a Facebook competition that celebrates your customer community

Your brand is an intangible asset that sits on your balance sheet. Finding ways to include creativity and rituals as well as ways to measure goals in your business will help to bring your brand to life. It should perpetually inspire your employees and entertain your customers.

Rituals create culture.

Chapter 10

HOW TO HIRE FOR YOUR LOGO DESIGN

What to look for when hiring a designer or branding agency

Make sure that when you choose a designer or branding agency that they ask you questions similar to the ones you have explored in this book. When you start with a clear brief for the graphic designer, you will avoid endless revisions, wasted time and frustration. It may take you extra time in the beginning when all you want is a logo design, but being clear early on will save you money and time in the long run. Awesome designers appreciate working with clients who think strategically about their brand, because it allows them to provide you their best possible work. It's up to the designer or branding agency to have a process in place to help you get clear before they start designing your new logo or naming your business.

As a startup, choosing a designer to work with is an important decision to make. If you want to develop a brand capable of becoming famous, I'd highly recommend choosing a designer that can grow with you. It's likely that you will not invest in having a brand guidelines document developed in the early days. In Chapter 7, we talked about the childhood telephone game and how we want to avoid any and all confusion with your brand signals. In my experience, if you work with several designers along the way chances are that each one of them will revise your brand just slightly. These refinements may look minimal to you now, because you are looking at your brand every day, but over time, all those small changes will add up to inconsistencies that may start to create confusion for the customer who is bombarded with messages and imagery every day. Protect your brand's consistency as though you're wearing a police badge. In the previous chapter, we talked about the five brand design elements that you want to protect.

There are three ways you may consider hiring a graphic designer: a freelance designer, an agency or, if you can afford it, you might want to hire a designer for your team. Generally the most affordable option is a freelance designer. If you want an agency to take you through a strategic process such as the one we have explored in this guidebook, it will usually start at around $30,000 USD to work with a small boutique firm. If you choose to work with a freelance designer you'll spend much less approximately $5,000 USD or less depending on how many years of experience they have.

Essentially, you need to match your business with the right designer. If you're developing a technology business, you'll need a designer with web design skills. On the other hand, if you are developing a restaurant you will need a designer who has experience with environmental design. If you are developing a consumer product you will need a designer who understands product packaging and so on. Ideally, you want to work with a graphic designer who has worked in or specializes in your business industry.

Questions to ask a graphic designer or branding agency before hiring them:

- What industries do they have the most experience working in? Here you are looking for industries that are the same or similar to your business.
- What core skills do they have as a designer(s)? For example: are they a web designer, packaging designer, print designer or environmental designer? If they say they do it all, ask them what they are most passionate about working on. You want to choose a designer that has the core skills you require.
- Ask to see their portfolio. Choose a few samples of their work that you like the most and ask probing questions about the ideas behind the designs. Then ask them how this idea fit with the client's strategy. You are looking for a designer that focuses their creative solutions in a way that works first and foremost for their clients. You don't want a designer that simply creates something that looks beautiful when you are building a brand.
- What information do they require from you? Most designers worth hiring will need information from you similar to the content we've explored in this book. If they don't have a process for capturing this important information from you then it's likely they are not taking a strategic approach to branding

your business

• Also, if you require items to be printed or packaged, ask them about their production experience. Alternatively, if you are an online business ask them about the best practices for making a website work as a business capture tool.

Why awesome designers don't join (most) crowdsourcing sites

When I came across a crowdsourcing design website for the first time, I was crowded around an iMac in Dubai with a group of brand designers and strategists poking fun at a certain website I won't mention. They said things like "giving your client 100 plus logo's isn't the point" and "what 'respectable' designer would ever join this site?" Granted, it was easy for them to say because they weren't footing the bills the multi-million dollar branding contracts our agency worked on. As I listened to them chat, I quietly realized to myself, that the creatives had a point, but so did this new crowdsourcing design industry.

Firstly, from the designers perspective, ethically participating on design pitches goes against designers greater conscious, because they see it as exploiting their time, expertise and artistic talent. After all, if you were going get a face lift or laser eye surgery you wouldn't wait to see if you liked the result before paying the doctor, would you? Creative pitches is something that graphic designers and branding agencies have been begrudgingly doing for decades in hopes of winning contracts. However, when expert creatives decide to participate in such pitch competitions they are very discerning about the fairness of the circumstance and want to know: 1) how many creative participants; and 2) if they are being compared to designers / agencies that have a similar of expertise.

Secondly, traditional crowdsourcing sites focus solely on the design solution, but expert graphic designers who specialize in branding know the value of creating a brand solution with an in-depth analysis of the business strategy for a company. Without it, a new logo design or visual solution is putting the cart before the horse. A creative solution alone is not going to address the business needs for a brand's long-term success. Traditional crowdsourcing websites promote the benefits of the quantity of how many logo designs their clients will get, when in fact this what that scares brand design experts away from participating on crowdsourcing sites.

Furthermore, when a client's brand is built on it's brand strategy the creative direction is very clear and the need for 100 logo's becomes irrelevant. Let's say you could afford to spend the minimum quarter of a million dollars to hire a globally recognized branding agency. Do you think they would present you 100 logo's? Absolutely, not. They would do something far more valuable. They would start the process with you by distilling your brand strategy and then presenting you only a few (not hundreds) of conceptual directions that aligned with the agreed strategic direction. They would show you a well thought through branding solution system with far more elements that just a logo design on a white background. You'd see the logic and emotional reasoning behind font selections, colour psychology, graphic devices, imagery style and how all of these elements come together and are applied to various branded touch point items such as print collateral, online, packaging and so on (discussed in the previous Chapter 9). Put another way, presenting 100 logo's would only serve to confuse the client because it would place all the attention on only one small detail of the brand (the logo design) when a successful brand needs to be a far more integrated solution.

It's common to see small businesses that focus purely on the aesthetic side of their brand changing their branding every few years towards the latest fad, but you'll notice that famous brands that act strategically like Apple, Patagonia and Whole Foods re-brand far they less often. In other words, they understand that branding without a strategy further perpetuates the intangible value of branding and fails to take full advantage of what a strategic solution can have for a company.

The pro's about crowdsourcing design

On the other hand, crowdsourcing has given birth to a whole new way of hiring a graphic designers, which has leveled the playing field for savvy entrepreneurs with big ideas to make the world a better place. What is missing are two key aspects: 1) a strategic approach to providing the designers the information they need to create long-term brand solutions; and 2) fair circumstances and an understanding for the designers needs to want to participate on crowdsourcing sites.

Provided the designers feel the pitch circumstances are kept fair they are far more likely to participate. Infact, when I launched Brands for the Heart , which is a hybrid between a strategic branding agency and a crowdsourcing design site, I interviewed graphic designers to understand exactly what business model they would be excited to join because I understood how valuable it would be to attract awesome designers like them. As a result, our business model was co-created based on the feedback we received from the very graphic designers who poo-pooed the crowdsourcing design industry around that iMac back in Dubai.

Thankfully, due to our holistic approach for both the designer and the entrepreneur we have created a business model that's a win-win for both the creative people and the business people.

Our branding packages include a logo, business card, home page design, font, colour and image palate and an item that the designer chooses starting at $595 and up, depending on the level of designer and design items you require. Plus, you will get access to Famous Brands 101 which is a do-it-yourself brand strategy training to help you get clear and feel confident. We match you with a graphic designer based on your budget along with the designer's core skills, industry experience and even the personality characteristics you desire. You will get matched with up to five designers from our hand picked community of designers from all over the world, including London, New York, LA, Perth, Vancouver, Toronto and more. These designers will then share their creative ideas with you for your brand brief. It's kind of like dating your designer first. If you are not happy with the creative concepts we will give you your money back-guaranteed.

www.ingramcontent.com/pod-product-compliance
Lightning Source LLC
LaVergne TN
LVHW040918150826
845672LV00007B/2107

* 9 7 9 8 4 5 9 5 2 7 9 8 8 *